Everything You Need to Know About *Teen Motherhood*

Although most teenage pregnancies are unintended, there is a lot that a young woman can do to prepare herself for motherhood.

Everything You Need to Know About *Teen Motherhood*

Jane Hammerslough

The Rosen Publishing Group, Inc.
New York

Published in 1990, 1992, 1995, 1997, 2001 by The Rosen Publishing Group, Inc.
29 East 21st Street, New York, NY 10010

Copyright © 1990, 1992, 1995, 1997, 2001 by The Rosen Publishing Group, Inc.

Revised Edition 2001

All rights reserved. No part of this book may be reproduced in any form without permission in writing from the publisher, except by a reviewer.

Library of Congress Cataloging-in-Publication Data

Hammerslough, Jane.
Everything you need to know about teen motherhood / Jane Hammerslough.—Revised ed.
(The need to know library)
Includes bibliographical references and index.
Summary: Discusses practical aspects of becoming a teenage mother, including what to do, how to do it, where to go for help, and what should be known about such topics as budgeting and baby care.
ISBN 978-1-4358-8766-4
1. Teenage mothers—United States—Juvenile literature. [1. Teenage parents. 2. Pregnancy.] I. Title. II. Series
HQ759.4.H36 1990
306.85'6—dc20

                                            89-39499
                                               CIP
                                                AC

Manufactured in the United States of America

Contents

	Introduction	6
Chapter 1	Tough Decisions	10
Chapter 2	Preparing for Motherhood	17
Chapter 3	Having a Baby	32
Chapter 4	The First Few Weeks	38
Chapter 5	Care for You and Your Baby: Questions and Answers	43
Chapter 6	Practical Decisions	49
Chapter 7	Prepare for Change	53
	Glossary	59
	Where to Go for Help	61
	For Further Reading	62
	Index	63

Introduction

The United States has the highest rates of teen pregnancy and births in the Western industrialized world. Four in ten young women become pregnant at least once before they reach the age of twenty—nearly one million a year. Eight in ten of these pregnancies are unintended, and 79 percent are to unmarried teens.

The teen birthrate declined slowly but steadily between 1991 and 1998 with an overall decline of 18 percent for those aged fifteen to nineteen. Preliminary data for 1999 show a 20 percent decline between 1991 and 1999. These recent declines reverse the 24 percent rise in the teenage birthrate from 1986 to 1991. Most teenagers who gave birth before 1980 were married, whereas most teenagers giving birth today are unmarried.

Part of the reason for the high rate of teenage pregnancy is that teens are becoming sexually active at younger ages. Half of all teenage boys and a third of all teenage girls today are sexually active. Teenagers get

Introduction

pregnant and decide to become mothers for a variety of reasons, from ignorance about sex to wanting to fill a void in their lives.

No matter why you choose to have your baby, the question of whether or not to become a mother is difficult. Every pregnant woman asks herself, "Am I ready to be a mother?" To answer that question, you need to answer other questions, such as:

- **Can I provide a safe home for my baby?**
- **Can I afford the costs of caring for my baby?**
- **How can I help my baby stay healthy, before and after it is born?**
- **How will a baby affect my goals or dreams?**

As a pregnant teenager, there are even more questions to ask yourself:

- **Why do I want to have this baby?**
- **Do I have people, such as parents or the father of the baby, to help me raise it?**
- **Will I be able to finish my education or training?**

It is important to think about these questions before your baby is born so that you will be able to make well-informed decisions about your future and that of your baby.

Teen Motherhood

Motherhood is a lifelong responsibility. Babies are completely dependent on their parents for all their needs. And as children grow, they continue to look to their parents for support and encouragement. Most of your time, energy, and money will be used to care for your child. You'll have far less time for yourself, your friends, and even for the father of the baby.

You have to be sure that you are ready to accept that kind of commitment. If you are unsure, talk to a trusted teacher, a counselor, a young mother, or your parents about what to expect and the options that are available to you.

Becoming a mother can be a wonderful experience. Mothers share a unique and special bond with their children. Despite the long hours and hard work, there is nothing more rewarding than seeing your baby's first smile or watching her take her first step.

The key to being a good mother is being prepared. This book will help you know what to expect while you're pregnant, and what to expect after the baby is born.

Watching your baby take his or her first steps will be one of the most rewarding experiences you will have as a new mother.

Chapter 1
Tough Decisions

Julia sat staring at the towels that hung from the back of the bathroom door. Even though she knew her parents were both at work, she had locked the door.

Since she'd felt so ill lately, she'd had little trouble convincing the school nurse that she needed to leave school early. On her way home, Julia had stopped by the drugstore and picked up a pregnancy test, praying that no one in the building would see her sneak up to her family's apartment.

Now she waited. She felt like waiting was all she'd been doing lately. Waiting for her period to come, waiting for Nick to call her back, waiting, now, for the results.

Her legs bounced up and down in silent rhythm. She glared at her watch. "Finally!" She closed her eyes, took a deep breath, and took two steps toward

Tough Decisions

the sink. On the counter, boldly spelled out in bright pink, the test showed she was pregnant.

Teen Pregnancy in the United States

One in every three teen mothers drops out of high school. With her education cut short, it is very difficult for a teen mother to find and keep a job. A teenage mother may become financially dependent on her family or on the government. Forty-eight percent of teens who become pregnant live in poverty.

Some 63 percent of teen parents depend on public programs for medical needs and daily living expenses, including formula, food, heat, and transportation. There are three million children under six being raised by teen parents or in alternative settings such as foster care or extended family situations. In every state, despite legislation that provides shelter for these young families, many teen parents and their children remain homeless.

The children of teenage mothers have lower birth weights and are more likely to perform poorly in school. The sons of teen mothers are 13 percent more likely to end up in prison, while daughters are 22 percent more likely to become teen mothers themselves.

Becoming a mother is a big responsibility. Seeking help and learning about the many issues involved will enable you to make smart decisions. It will better prepare you for your new role as a young parent.

Many teenagers feel a sense of fear and guilt when they find out that they are pregnant.

Tough Decisions

Smart Choices

Most girls who learn they are pregnant feel a number of emotions: fear, confusion, uncertainty. The decision to become a parent is one of the biggest decisions you will make in your life. Think carefully about how that choice will affect you now and in the future.

Most teen girls become pregnant by accident, like Julia did. But some choose to have and raise their babies. There are many complicated and varied reasons for making this important decision. Some teens believe that having the baby will solve problems with their parents or make them adults. Some feel it will make them more important in the eyes of their friends and family. Others like the idea of having someone to care for and love. But having a baby will accomplish none of these things.

Special Needs

You have special needs when you are pregnant. You have different needs once your baby is born. Your baby will have many special needs, too. It is important to learn what these needs are and how best to meet them.

When you are pregnant, your body changes. You need to eat certain foods to help your baby grow properly. You also need special medical care. It is very important for you to stay healthy during your pregnancy for the sake of your baby.

Teen Motherhood

You and your baby need a safe, secure place to live. You need money to pay for the baby's expenses. You may also need to find child care so you can go to work. Your financial needs will change when you become a mother. You now need to think about what is best for two people: you and the baby.

Almost all expectant and new mothers need personal support. Pregnancy can make you moody and upset, no matter how happy you are about having a baby. Being a new mother can be scary. It will help if you can talk about your worries and needs with someone who cares. You can get support from your family, the baby's father, your friends, your guidance counselor, or teachers.

While you are pregnant, it is important to think about what you'll need and how to get it. Consider these sources of support:

Your Family

If you are a single parent, will your parents let you and your child live at home? Will they give you money for things the baby needs? Can they help you when you need help? It is important to think about whether your family can offer support.

Sometimes, your parents want you to raise a baby because they want a grandchild. But you must think of yourself and your baby first. Can you and your parents agree on the best way to raise a child? Will you feel trapped? Will you have trouble moving out or marrying

Your baby is ultimately your responsibility, no matter how supportive your parents are.

in the future? If something happened to your parents, would you be able to take care of a child yourself?

The Father

Even if you never were or no longer are in a relationship, it is important to inform the father of your baby of your pregnancy. Talk about the desires, fears, and future plans that each of you have. Make choices that will help each of you reach your goals. Ideally, you should see a counselor and discuss your options together. However, you and the father may not be able to come to a decision on which you can both agree. Whatever your decision, he has a legal financial obligation to your baby.

Teen Motherhood

Professional Support

Getting support from someone who isn't involved in your decision can be very helpful. You can talk with a teacher or counselor about your feelings. They may help you think things through more clearly.

Remember that you are a source of support for yourself. Be honest about your own desires, fears, and choices. If the father is not part of your life, how do you feel about being a single parent, about your child growing up without a father, about your family taking part (or not taking part) in raising your child? Thinking about these things will help you make the best decision for yourself.

Chapter 2
Preparing for Motherhood

Your body goes through many changes when you are pregnant. You are important to your baby before it is even born. When you decide to become a mother, it is important to get medical care as soon as possible. You can go to a local health clinic for care.

Prenatal Care

Prenatal means "before birth." Prenatal care is very important for your own health and the health of the baby. This means going to see a midwife or a doctor who delivers babies as soon as you can. This special kind of doctor is called an obstetrician. A midwife is not a doctor, but she is trained to care for expectant mothers and to deliver babies.

Teen Motherhood

Pregnancy lasts for nine months. A midwife or obstetrician will usually see you once a month for the first seven months. After that, you will go every two weeks. At the very end of your pregnancy, you will go each week.

Your weight and blood pressure will be checked at each visit. The doctor or midwife will also measure you to make sure your baby is growing well. After the fourth month, you may be able to listen to your baby's heartbeat.

Your Developing Baby

Month One
For the first eight weeks, your developing baby is called an embryo. The embryo looks like a tadpole. Heart and lungs are beginning to form. By day twenty-five, the heart starts to beat. The neural tube, which becomes the brain and spinal cord, begins to form. At the end of the first month, the embryo is about half an inch long and weighs less than an ounce.

Month Two
All major body organs and systems are formed, but they are not yet completely developed. Early stages of the placenta, which exchanges nutrients from your body for waste products produced by the baby, are visible and working. Ears, ankles, and wrists are formed. Fingers and toes are developed. By the end of

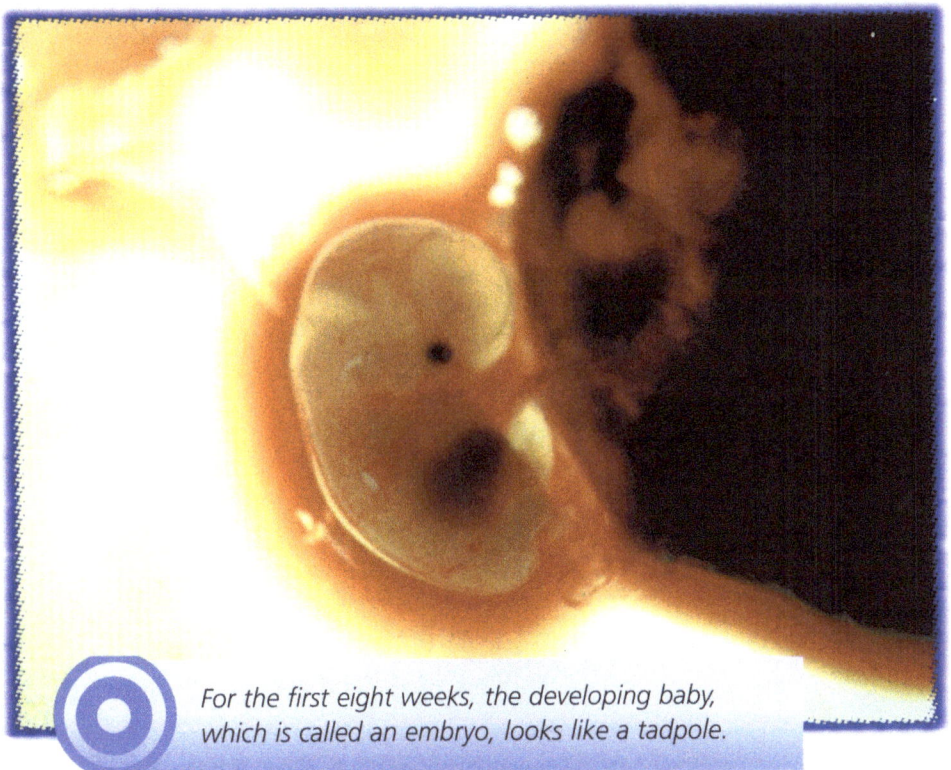

For the first eight weeks, the developing baby, which is called an embryo, looks like a tadpole.

the second month, the embryo looks more like a person than a tadpole. The embryo is about one inch long, and still weighs less than an ounce.

Month Three

After eight weeks as an embryo, the baby is called a fetus. The fetus's fingers and toes develop soft nails. By the end of this month, the fetus is four inches long and weighs a little over an ounce. The first trimester is over at the end of the third month.

Month Four

The fetus moves, kicks, swallows, and can hear your voice. The umbilical cord continues to grow and thicken to carry enough nourishment from mother to fetus—but it can also pass along hazards like tobacco, alcohol, and other drugs. The placenta is now fully formed. By the end of this month, the fetus is six to seven inches long and weighs about five ounces.

Month Five

The fetus becomes more active now, turning from side to side and sometimes head over heels. The fetus now sleeps and wakes at regular intervals. This is a month of rapid growth; at the end of the fifth month, the fetus is eight to twelve inches long and weighs between eight ounces and one pound.

Month Six

The fetus continues its rapid growth. The fetus's skin is wrinkled and covered with fine, soft hair. The eyelids begin to part and the eyes open during this month. Fingerprints and toeprints can be seen. At the end of the sixth month, the fetus is eleven to fourteen inches long and weighs one and a half pounds.

Month Seven

By the end of the twenty-eighth week, the fetus weighs about two and a half to three pounds and measures about fourteen to sixteen inches long. A slick, white, fatty substance covers the skin. The eyes open and close, and the fetus may suck his or her thumb.

Preparing for Motherhood

Month Eight
Rapid brain growth continues. The fetus is too big now to move around much but can kick strongly and roll. You may notice the shape of an elbow or heel through your abdomen. The bones of the head are soft and flexible to make it easier for the baby to fit through the birth canal. The lungs may still be immature. The fetus is now about eighteen inches long and weighs about five pounds.

Month Nine
At thirty-eight to forty weeks, your baby is full-term. The baby's lungs are mature and ready to function on their own. During this month, the baby gains about half a pound a week. The baby usually "drops" into a head-down position and rests lower in the mother's abdomen. By the end of the ninth month, the baby weighs six to nine pounds and is nineteen to twenty-one inches long.

How You May Feel

Pregnancy lasts about forty weeks. Each three-month period is called a trimester. There are three trimesters in each pregnancy. Being pregnant is a big change for your body. Here are some ways you might feel different during each trimester.

The First Trimester
At the start of this trimester, your period will stop. Your breasts will be slightly bigger and sore. You may

have morning sickness, cravings, or hate foods you usually like. You will urinate more often because your growing uterus is pressing on your bladder.

By the second month, the area around your nipples may begin to darken. Morning sickness may continue. You may feel tired and need to rest more as your body adjusts to being pregnant. The total amount of blood in your body increases. You may notice that you've become irritable or moody.

Supplement your diet with the B-vitamin folic acid (it's found in most multivitamins) to reduce the risk of birth defects of the brain and spine. By the end of the first trimester, you may have gained three or four pounds. Visit your health care provider for your first prenatal care checkup as soon as you think you are pregnant. Ask your health care provider before taking any prescription drugs or over-the-counter products.

The Second Trimester

Your appetite increases now as morning sickness goes away. You begin to feel more energetic. Toward the end of the fourth month (16–20 weeks), you might feel the faint movement of your baby for the first time; tell your health care provider when you do. Your belly begins to show—you will probably need maternity clothes and bigger bras this month.

Pregnant women need extra iron—more than even a good diet can supply. Your doctor may recommend

Preparing for Motherhood

iron supplements. You'll probably gain about one pound a week, or twelve to fourteen pounds, during the second trimester.

Your uterus will grow to the height of your belly button. Your heart will beat faster. You may need eight hours of sleep each night. Take rest breaks during the day if you feel tired; don't push yourself. You may get leg cramps, especially at night, if you are not getting enough calcium.

Before the second trimester ends, you will feel the fetus kicking more strongly. The skin on your growing belly may start to itch. Your back may hurt. Wear low-heeled shoes or flats. Exercise can also help prevent backaches. Don't stand for long periods of time. You may feel pain down the side of your belly as your uterus stretches.

The Third Trimester

You are in the homestretch now! If your ankles and feet swell from standing, lie down with your feet raised. If swelling lasts longer than twenty-four hours, or if your hands or feet swell suddenly, call your health care provider. Stretch marks may appear on your abdomen and breasts as they get bigger. You may feel false labor contractions, also called Braxton Hicks contractions. This is normal, but call your health care provider if you have more than five contractions in one hour. As your belly gets bigger, you may lose your sense of balance and feel clumsy.

Teen Motherhood

You may experience some leakage of colostrum (the fluid that will feed your baby until your milk comes in) from your breasts as they begin to produce milk. You may have trouble sleeping because it's hard to get comfortable. You may develop shortness of breath as the baby crowds your lungs. The baby may also crowd your stomach; try eating five or six smaller meals during the day.

Your belly button may stick out. Your breathing should be easier once the baby "drops," but you'll have to urinate more often because it's pressing on your bladder. Your cervix will open up (dilate) and thin out (efface) as it prepares for birth. You may be very uncomfortable because of the pressure and weight of the fetus. Be sure to rest often.

Call your health care provider right away if you have:

- Bleeding or a gush of fluid from your vagina
- Cramps
- Stomach pains
- A dull backache
- Blurry vision
- Spots before your eyes
- A feeling that the baby is pushing down

Preparing for Motherhood

- A decrease in your baby's movements
- More than five contractions in one hour

Exercise

Some women find that light to moderate exercise during the first and second trimesters can help get rid of some discomfort. It also gives them more energy. Ask your doctor or midwife whether it is okay for you to exercise.

What to Eat

It is important for you to eat the right foods when you are pregnant. This is especially important for teen mothers because as a teen, you are still growing. You and your baby need good food and the right nutrients to develop properly. It is important to eat good, fresh foods. Junk food will not help you or the baby.

You should gain weight slowly and steadily when you are pregnant. It is best to gain between twenty and thirty pounds. Do not starve yourself because you feel fat. Being fat and being pregnant are very different. The weight that you gain during your pregnancy comes off relatively easily after you have the baby. You can give your baby the best start by following these suggestions about what to eat:

Light to moderate exercise is usually good for both mother and baby.

Protein

You should have four servings of protein foods a day. They help your baby grow. Here are some examples of good protein foods. Each of these is one serving.

- 3 cups of milk
- 3/4 cup of cottage cheese, 2–3 ounces of hard cheese
- 2 eggs
- 2–3 ounces of tuna, chicken, turkey, fish, lean beef, pork, veal, lamb, liver, or shellfish
- 1 cup of black or other dried beans

Preparing for Motherhood

- 5 ounces of tofu
- 4 tablespoons of peanut butter

It is best to have fresh, homemade food. Avoid fast food, fried food, and food that is high in fat or sugar. Broiling and baking are much healthier than frying. Good high-protein snacks include nuts and whole-grained baked goods.

Calcium-Rich Foods

These foods help your baby's bones develop. They also help keep your teeth in good shape. Have four servings every day of these foods.

- 8 ounces of milk, 1 3/4 cups cottage cheese, or 1 cup yogurt (this can also count as part of your daily protein)
- 2 ounces of hard cheese
- 3–4 ounces of canned salmon, mackerel, or sardines with bones
- 2–3 tablespoons sesame seeds
- 2/3 cup of collard greens
- 1 1/4 cup of fresh kale, mustard, or turnip greens
- 1 1/2 cups of broccoli
- 2–3 tablespoons molasses
- 2–3 ounces almonds

Vegetables and Fruits

Have two to three servings each day. One serving should be raw, as cooking can destroy vitamins.

Whole Grains and Carbohydrates

Have four to five servings daily.

- 1 slice whole-wheat bread
- 1/2 cup cooked rice
- 1/2 cup cooked cereal, such as Wheatena
- 1/2 cup whole-grain cold cereal (like Shredded Wheat)
- 1/2 cup cooked pasta

During your pregnancy you will need more iron. Eating dried fruits, liver, beef, and spinach can give you more iron. You also need vitamin C. Have a glass of citrus juice (orange or grapefruit) or a fresh orange, strawberries, grapefruit, tomatoes, or a green pepper every day. Also, remember to drink plenty of liquids when you are pregnant. The best are water, juice, and herbal teas.

Fats

Your body also needs small amounts of fat each day. You can get this in oil, butter, margarine, mayonnaise, or cream. Don't overdo it. You don't want to gain too much weight.

Teen mothers and their babies need good, fresh foods and the right nutrients to develop properly.

What to Avoid When You Are Pregnant

Everything that you take into your body when you are pregnant will affect your baby. Some things, such as protein and vitamins, will have good effects. Other things, such as junk food, cigarettes, and drugs, will have bad effects. To be sure you give your baby the best chance to be healthy, avoid these things:

- **Cigarettes** Smoking will increase the risk of losing your baby during pregnancy. It can also cause low birth weight in babies. Nicotine and carbon monoxide

Teen Motherhood

keep your baby from getting the food and oxygen he or she needs to grow. Babies born to smokers are often sickly and need extra hospital care. Some are born too early; others may die at birth or within the first year.

- **Drugs** Many drugs are dangerous to your unborn baby. This includes illegal, over-the-counter, and herbal drugs. He or she is still developing and is very fragile. If you are addicted to a drug, your baby will often be born addicted. Always check with your doctor or midwife before you take any drug.

- **Caffeine** Too much caffeine is bad during pregnancy. Limit yourself to one cup of tea, coffee, or caffeinated soda per day.

- **Alcohol** If you drink alcohol while pregnant, you put your baby at risk. He or she may be born addicted or with severe mental and physical birth defects.

Teenagers who smoke during pregnancy run the risk of harming their babies.

Chapter 3

Having a Baby

The process of having a baby is called childbirth. It can be intense and exciting. It can also be scary. It is best if you understand what happens to your body during childbirth.

Many doctors and midwives believe that relaxing during childbirth is important. You can learn to relax in prepared childbirth classes. One type of class is called Lamaze (Lah-MAHZ).

In Lamaze classes you learn ways of breathing that help you relax. You and a "coach" practice together. Your coach can be the baby's father, someone in your family, or a friend. Some classes offer discussion groups, films on giving birth, and visits to the hospital where you will deliver. Ask your obstetrician or midwife about Lamaze classes.

Having a Baby

Preparing for Labor and Delivery

Preparing yourself for labor and delivery will help you feel more relaxed and composed once the process actually begins. Be sure to do the following well in advance of your due date:

- If you plan to give birth at a hospital or birthing center, find out if you need to preregister.
- If you are working, make arrangements for your maternity leave.
- Obtain your health care provider's phone number so you can reach him or her for any emergency that occurs after office hours.
- If you will need transportation to a hospital or birth center, establish who will drive you and how you will contact the person when labor starts.
- Decide how you will feed your baby and what supplies you may need.
- If you plan to deliver at a hospital or birth center, contact them to see what personal items you will need to pack for yourself. You'll probably want a comfortable gown or robe, toiletries,

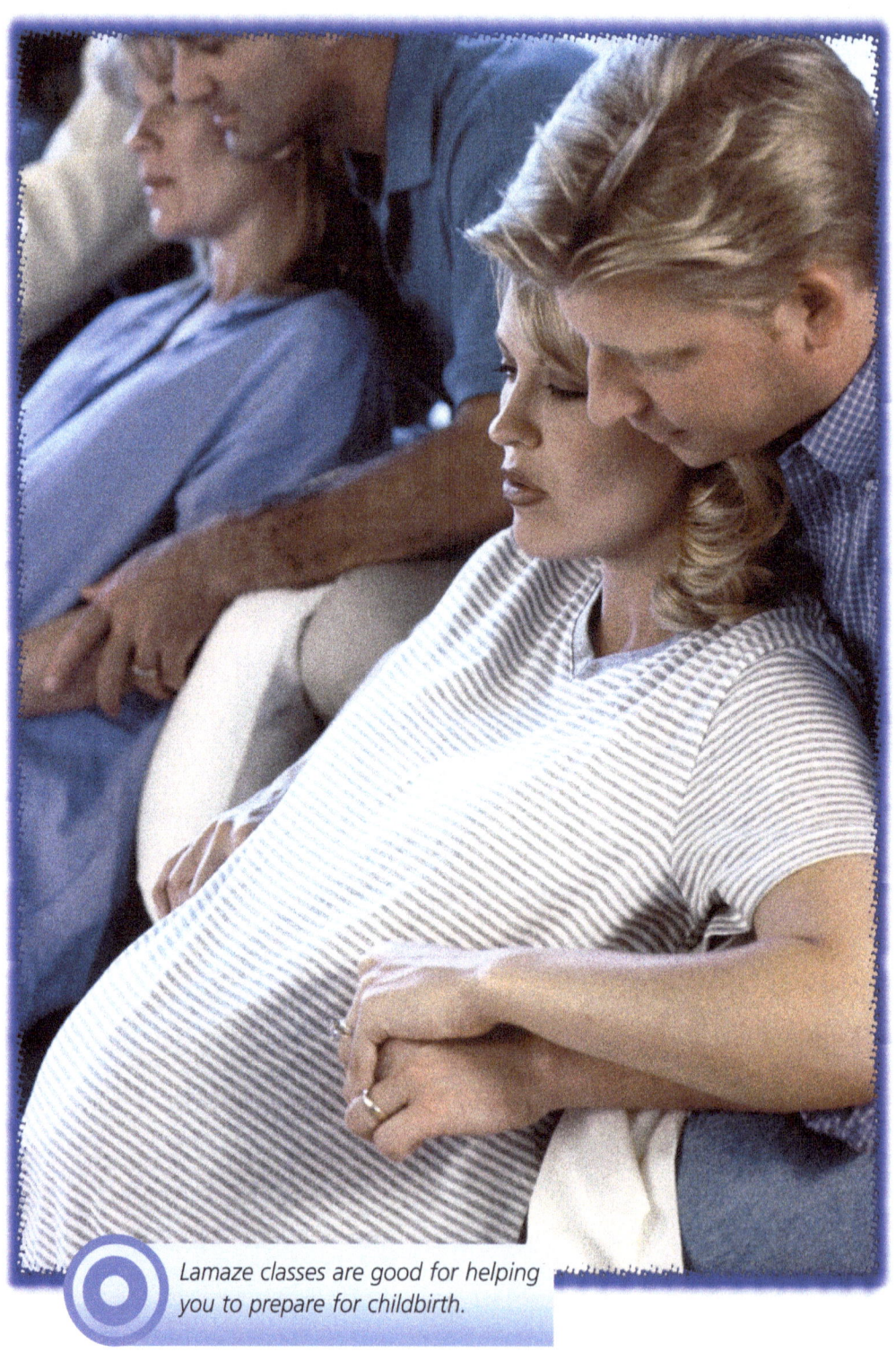

Lamaze classes are good for helping you to prepare for childbirth.

Having a Baby

sanitary napkins, nursing supplies, a camera with film and batteries, and important phone numbers. You will also need clothes for yourself and your baby for the trip home.

Stages of Childbirth

Labor

The first part of childbirth is called labor. It is called labor because it is hard work. During labor, your uterus prepares to give birth. Your uterus is where your baby has lived for the last nine months. Your cervix is the entryway from the uterus into the birth canal. During labor, your cervix opens up. The doctor or midwife will say that you are dilating. Labor occurs in three stages. The first is called early labor.

Early Labor

Early labor is the longest and least intense phase of labor. It can last from a few hours to several days. During early labor, you will feel contractions. Contractions feel like squeezes inside of you. They last thirty to forty-five seconds. You may feel some cramps, indigestion, or diarrhea. You may also have "bloody show," a pink discharge from your vagina. When contractions are five minutes apart, you should go to the hospital.

Active Labor

Active labor is the second phase. This phase can last two to four hours. Contractions are stronger and more frequent. This means your body is preparing for delivery. Breathing exercises can help you relax during this phase. You may feel pain or dizziness.

Transitional Labor

Transitional labor is the last and shortest phase of labor. Your contractions are two to three minutes apart and become very strong. They last for sixty to ninety seconds. Transitional labor can last from fifteen minutes to an hour. You may feel very tired and find it hard to relax.

Pushing and Delivery

Pushing and delivery is the second part of childbirth. It begins when your cervix is open wide enough for a baby's head. This part of childbirth can last anywhere from ten minutes to three hours.

You will continue to have contractions during this stage. Your obstetrician or midwife will tell you when to push. Sometimes, pushing can be very intense. Usually a baby's head comes out first. Pushing the baby out is called delivery.

Delivery of Placenta

The final part of childbirth is delivery of the placenta. The placenta is where your baby lived inside the uterus.

Having a Baby

You push out the placenta. It can take between five minutes to half an hour.

Cesarean Births

Sometimes, a baby must be delivered through surgery. This is called a cesarean section delivery, and it is not uncommon. During a cesarean, the doctor makes an incision (a cut) and removes the baby surgically through your abdomen. Anesthesia makes you go to sleep before the procedure so you will not feel any pain.

Sometimes, you have a cesarean delivery because the baby is in trouble and must be delivered quickly. Sometimes, it is safer for the mother to have the baby by cesarean.

Postnatal Care

Postnatal means "after birth." You will receive postnatal care in the hospital after you've given birth.

Many new mothers are very happy and tired after delivery. Depending on the policy of your hospital, you may or may not be able to hold your baby right away. In any case, it will not be long before you can see your baby.

You may stay in the hospital for a day or more after the birth. With a cesarean you will stay in the hospital longer. You will be examined each day by your obstetrician or midwife. You may feel some soreness after having your baby.

Chapter 4: The First Few Weeks

The first few days after the birth may be difficult. You will probably feel some pain, and you may be very tired. Get plenty of rest during and after your hospital stay.

It will also take time to get used to having your baby at home. You may be uncertain at first about your baby's needs. It is helpful to keep your doctor's or your parents' phone number in a convenient place if you have questions or in case of an emergency. The obstetrics department at your hospital can also answer questions. If possible, it is a good idea to have someone experienced around the house after the birth to help you take care of the baby and the household chores.

Your mood may also change soon after you give birth. You may feel sad or anxious, even though you are

The First Few Weeks

glad to have a baby. These feelings, called postpartum depression, are normal. Many new mothers experience them, but they usually disappear in a few weeks. If not, speak with a counselor or your doctor.

Caring for an Infant

Taking care of a newborn means doing many different tasks. Feeding, bathing, diapering, and holding are just a few of the things mothers need to know. These things are not hard to learn, but they do take a little practice.

Holding Your Baby

A newborn's neck is not strong. Also, newborn babies have a soft spot on the top of their heads called a fontanel. Be careful of this soft spot when you handle the baby. After about a year, the fontanel becomes hard.

Feeding Your Baby

Babies need to eat often, especially during the first few weeks. You will need to decide on the method to feed your baby. Most mothers can choose between breast-feeding and bottle-feeding.

Breast-Feeding

Breast-feeding is the most natural method of feeding. You produce milk that is pure and at the right temperature, and your milk contains the nutrients a baby needs. There is nothing to buy. It is all there, ready when needed. Your milk also contains your antibodies.

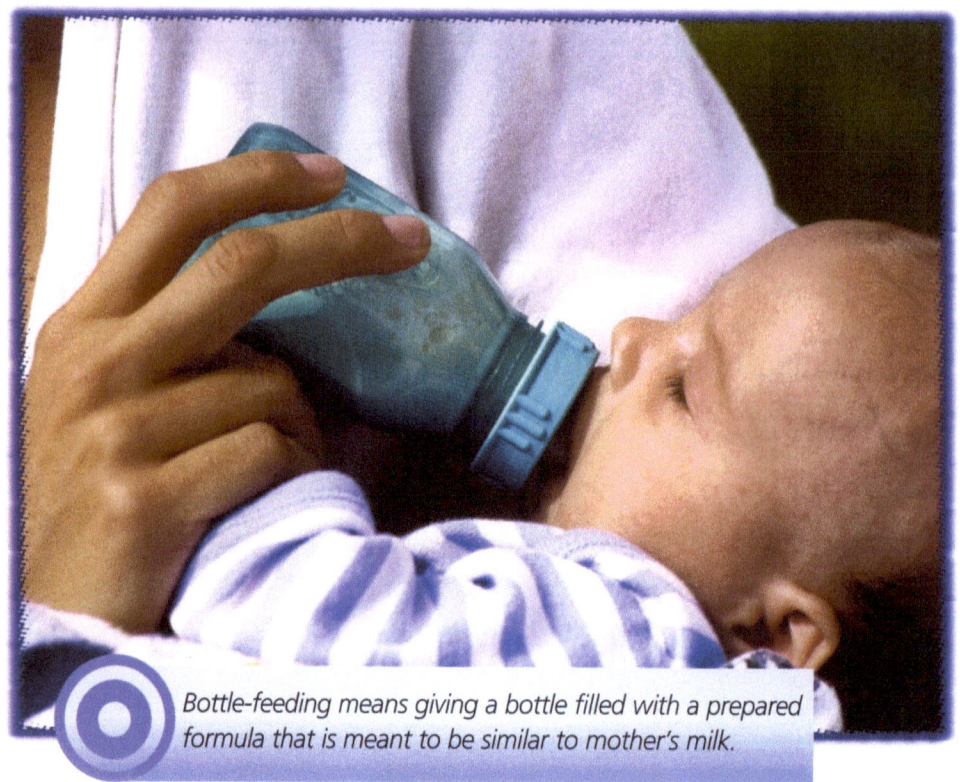

Bottle-feeding means giving a bottle filled with a prepared formula that is meant to be similar to mother's milk.

Antibodies are natural chemicals in your body that protect the baby from certain infections. When you breast-feed, you should continue with your pregnancy diet. You should drink plenty of liquids as well. Breast-feeding burns many calories.

Bottle-Feeding

Bottle-feeding means giving a baby a bottle filled with formula. Today, most mothers use prepared formulas that are meant to be similar to mother's milk. You can buy formula in most drugstores and supermarkets. Bottle-feeding is much more expensive than breast-feeding, and it can take time to prepare.

The First Few Weeks

Some new mothers decide to breast-feed for a few months and then use a combination of breast-feeding and formula feeding. Doing this can help you have the advantages of both methods. Both breast-feeding and bottle-feeding can help you to bond with your baby. Bonding is a feeling of closeness. It makes a baby feel loved.

Most mothers feed their babies on demand, when they seem hungry. A baby may cry after eating because he or she needs to burp. Babies swallow a lot of air by sucking when they feed. All this air can hurt their stomachs. Hold the baby upright against your chest and gently rub or pat its back.

Sleeping

Newborn babies sleep a lot of the time. After you feed and burp your baby, it is a good idea to put him or her in a crib. That way the baby will get used to the idea of sleeping after eating.

Diapers

A few days after your baby is born, it will produce a very dark stool (bowel movement) called meconium. This is normal. Sometimes babies cry because their diapers are wet or cold. Wet diapers can also cause diaper rash. Diaper rash can be painful for your baby. It is best to check and change diapers often.

Most mothers choose between cloth diapers and disposables. Cloth diapers are easy to use with diaper covers and can be picked up, washed, and delivered by a diaper service. Disposable diapers can be very convenient, but they are expensive. They also create much garbage that strains the environment.

Baths

You can give your baby a bath every day. At first it can be scary to give a baby a tub bath because the tub is very slippery. You can start with sponge baths for a few weeks and work up to tub baths.

You can give a bath in a dishpan or small tub in a warm place. The water should be about body temperature and feel comfortably warm. Before you start, set a towel aside for drying the baby. Support the baby's back and head with one arm while you soap the baby with the other. Use only an inch or two of water until you get used to giving baths. You need to wash the baby's scalp only once or twice a week.

Chapter 5

Care for You and Your Baby: Questions and Answers

After a few months, you will get to know your baby. You will become more confident about taking care of your baby. You will start to learn what he or she likes and needs. But all new mothers have questions about their babies. Here are some of the questions that new mothers often ask:

Help! My baby won't stop crying! What should I do?

In the beginning, some babies don't cry much at all. Some cry often. You can try feeding the baby, changing it, turning it over, singing to it, or just holding it. Doing these things may help. Sometimes, though, a baby just won't stop crying.

Constant crying can be caused by colic. Colic causes sharp pains in your baby's intestines after eating. You can tell the difference between hungry crying and colic. A baby who is hungry cries before eating, not after.

Colic may be relieved by burping the baby, rocking it gently, rubbing its back, or giving it a pacifier. Nobody is sure what causes colic.

As a mother, colic can make you mad when nothing you try seems to help. Fortunately, it usually goes away when the baby is around three months old.

Can I spoil my baby by holding it too often?

No. In the first few months, it's important to hold your baby often. Holding and talking to your baby lets the baby know that you love him or her. The baby begins to learn that you will be there when it needs you.

My baby is driving me crazy, and I feel trapped. What should I do?

If you feel upset, it is always best to talk to somebody about it. Talk to a counselor, a friend, or your family about your feelings. If you feel very angry toward your baby, count to ten. See if you can find a baby-sitter and go out by yourself for an hour. If you can take time to calm down you won't take your frustration out on your baby.

Your baby is helpless and doesn't understand that his or her crying may upset you. Child abuse is a very serious problem. Never, ever hit an infant for any reason. Hitting your baby is child abuse.

Since I gave birth, I've been bleeding. Is this normal?

Yes. For a week or two after birth, new mothers discharge lochia, which is similar to having your period. If

Care for You and Your Baby: Questions and Answers

heavy bleeding lasts longer than that, speak to your health care practitioner.

Do I need to see a doctor after I have my baby?

Yes. Arrange to see your obstetrician, midwife, or gynecologist for a checkup six weeks after delivery. At this time, you will be given an internal exam. Since pregnancy is possible during these early weeks, you may want to discuss birth control with your health care professional at the time of your checkup. It's important to plan when and if you want another child.

When should I take my baby to the doctor?

Your baby will need to see a doctor two weeks after birth and every month or so for the first year. A doctor who cares for infants and young children is called a pediatrician. Good baby care is important to your baby's health. Your baby will need a series of shots. These shots protect a baby from diseases. The doctor will also check your baby's weight and length. Later, your baby will still have regular checkups, but less often.

Ask your pediatrician questions about your baby's health and development. If you are concerned about something, talk to your doctor.

My baby has a rash. What should I do?

Call your pediatrician. Some rashes are common, like diaper rash. Rough or bumpy red patches in the diaper area are a sign of diaper rash. It can be caused by

Teen Motherhood

wetness. If there is a rash, do not use plastic pants, which keep in moisture. Wash the area carefully and rinse soap off twice with clear water. (If left on the skin, soap can make the problem worse.) Other kinds of rashes may be a sign of allergies or illness, and should be checked.

Why does my baby's scalp look dirty, even though I wash it?

Your baby may have cradle cap, which is a crusty irritation of the scalp. Cradle cap is very common in the early months of life. Daily washing with soap and water may help. The condition disappears after a few months.

My baby is cranky and keeps pulling on both ears. Is she okay?

Call your pediatrician as soon as possible. Your baby may have an ear infection. This is common in infants and painful for them. Your doctor can give your baby medicine to prevent damage to her hearing.

Emergencies

It is a good idea to keep a list of important phone numbers by your phone. You should call your pediatrician immediately if your baby:

- **Is vomiting with great force more than once a day**
- **Eats any drug or object by mistake**

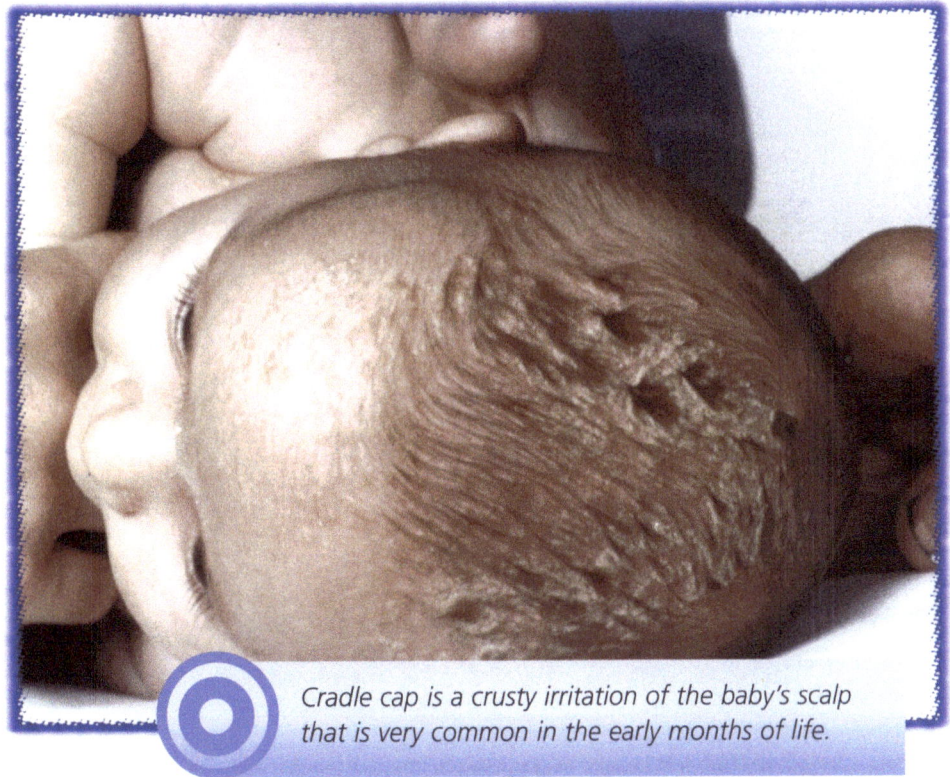

Cradle cap is a crusty irritation of the baby's scalp that is very common in the early months of life.

- **Seems to be having trouble breathing or is choking**
- **Seems to be sick or has a temperature**

Development

It is always a good idea for parents to pay attention to their baby's physical development. That means watching to see that your baby is alert, can focus his or her eyes, and has some coordination. It is important to remember that all babies develop at their own rate. Each baby will have his or her own schedule for development. The list that follows will give you an idea about some of the things most babies do in the first six months. If your baby does not do all these things, there is no cause for alarm. Just keep paying attention. If you become concerned, you should tell your doctor what you're worried about.

Baby's First Six Months: What Happens When?

- 1 month: Grasps finger; pushes out arms and legs; responds to touch
- 2 months: Follows movement with eyes; hands open more; shows emotions; soothed by voice and touch
- 3 months: Cries less; smiles; can lean on elbows while on stomach
- 4 months: Can hold on to objects, puts them in mouth; laughs; can lift head
- 5 months: Rolls from stomach to back; smiles and babbles for attention; head steady; enjoys touching and tasting objects
- 6 months: Sits with support; turns head; makes many sounds to express excitement, delight, or fear; can hold bottle

Chapter 6

Practical Decisions

Your decision to become a mother involves practical choices. These include where you'll live, how you will support yourself and your baby, how to continue your education, and where to find child care.

Where You'll Live

You and your baby must have a safe, secure place to live. Some teenage girls who are pregnant can choose where they want to live. Some have only one alternative. Reaching a decision on where you and your baby will live can sometimes be tough.

To make the best choice, you might ask yourself questions like these:

- **Is it a good place for an infant? Is there enough space, light, and quiet?**

- Do you get along with the people you will live with? Will they take advantage of you?

- What kind of contribution will you be able to make to the household? If necessary, will you be able to work to help out with expenses?

- Will someone else at home be available at times to help you take care of the baby?

Your Expenses

Becoming a mother involves many expenses. A crib or a stroller is a one-time expense. Other expenses, like food and clothing, continue. To give your baby the best start in life, learning about these expenses is important.

Many teenage mothers have problems with money. Most live at a low income level. Some public assistance is available. Call your local department of social services for more information on getting welfare. You can also call them about receiving food stamps.

It is better to have other sources of income, if possible. It is also best to finish high school as soon as you can. People with high school diplomas have a much better chance of earning a higher income.

Practical Decisions

Government Programs

Several government programs exist at the national and local level to promote the economic and social health of children and their families. Ask your health care provider or visit your local social service agency to find out what programs are offered in your community.

Women, Infants, Children (WIC)

WIC provides some low-income, nutritionally at-risk pregnant women and their children with food, nutrition education, counseling at WIC clinics, and screening and referrals to other health, welfare, and social services.

Temporary Assistance for Needy Families (TANF)

TANF provides assistance and work opportunities to needy families and grants states federal funds to develop and define their own assistance programs. These programs have different names and application processes from state to state. The Office of Family Assistance (OFA) oversees TANF. Again, consult your local social service agency to find out if you qualify and how to apply.

The Child Support Enforcement Program

Your baby's father is legally financially responsible for your baby. If he is unwilling to help you, you can find out how to enroll in government programs such as the Child Support Enforcement Program. The goal of the program is to ensure that parents assume financial responsibility for any children that they have, whether or not these children are born within marriage. The current services of the program include establishing paternity, or the father's identity, for all children born out of wedlock, and setting and enforcing child support orders for all children who have a parent not living with them.

Child Care

If you work, you will probably need child care. Ask your family, friends, and neighbors if they know anyone who can help. If you find someone this way, make sure you trust the person with your baby.

You can also call the Agency for Child Development in your area to find out about government-run day care programs. If one of your friends also has a baby, you might arrange to share or trade baby-sitting services.

Chapter 7

Prepare for Change

Think about the things you will need for a baby now and in the future. Having a budget gives you a good idea of how much money you need. It helps you decide which expenses are most important. Figure out how much each thing costs and write it down on paper.

Basic Expenses

- Apartment (security deposit and rent)
- Heat
- Electricity
- Laundry
- Telephone (hookup and monthly charges)
- Food (for self and baby)
- Clothing (for self and baby)

Teen Motherhood

- Child care
- Health care and insurance
- Transportation (buses, etc.)
- Car (payments and insurance)
- Social life (movies, restaurants, etc.)
- Savings

Talk to people who already have their own apartments. That way you can find out how much you might spend per month on these things. Discuss your needs for food and clothing costs with a counselor or with another parent.

To plan a budget, add up the cost each month of all items that are necessities. Then make a list of the optional items and what they cost. Subtract these totals from your expected monthly income.

It is important to be able to live on your income. If your basic expenses are less than your income, good. You can use the leftover money for your optional expenses and savings. Are your basic expenses greater than your income? Then you will need help.

Other Expenses

You need bedding, clothing, and feeding and bathing equipment for your baby. Fortunately, you can borrow many of these things or buy them secondhand.

Prepare for Change

Clothing

It will make your life easier to get simple, loose-fitting clothing. Your baby will grow very quickly during the first year. So buy the three- to six-month size only if the baby is small.

- Diapers: four dozen if you wash them yourself; a dozen "spares" if you use a diaper service; two dozen disposable diapers for day trips, visiting, etc.
- T-Shirts: four to six
- Waterproof pants: three or four (If you use only disposables, you won't need these.)
- Sleepers: three or four (sleeping "sacks," with a bottom tie or zipper, to keep baby's feet snug).
- Stretch suits: three or four.
- Receiving blankets: three or four (to keep your newborn baby snug and comfortable when going out).
- Sweaters: one or two.
- Blanket sleeper.
- Booties or socks.
- Outer clothing, such as snow suit (if you live in a cold climate).

Feeding Equipment

- Breast-feeding is generally more economical than feeding a baby formula. If you eat properly, your milk will be perfect food for your baby.
- Bottles: if breast-feeding, two or three for water and juice; if feeding formula, eight or nine (eight-ounce size).
- Mixing container marked in ounces (for formula).
- Extra nipples.
- Bottle brush.
- Pot or kettle for sterilizing bottles.

Bedding

You will not need a crib right away. In the beginning you can even use a box if you need to. Be sure it is cushioned for the baby to sleep in with soft padding. It is best not to use a pillow.

- Crib and mattress
- Mattress pads: two or three
- Bumper
- Waterproof sheets: two or three
- Comforter

Prepare for Change

- Fitted crib sheets: two or three

Bathing Equipment

- Plastic tub for bathing
- Washcloths and towels
- Blunt-edged nail scissors
- Petroleum jelly (Vaseline)

Other Equipment

- Changing table
- Diaper pail
- Snuggler
- Stroller and auto safety seat

Changes

Right now, you may live at home. You may work part-time. You go to school. You probably have a lot of time for yourself and your friends. All of this will change once your baby is born. You will be a mother. You will be responsible for the care and safety of your baby. Your role in your family will change. Your parents may have a hard time adjusting to the fact that you are a parent.

Your friendships will probably also be different after you have a baby. Becoming a mother takes a lot of time.

Teen Motherhood

It is tiring. You probably won't spend as much time with your friends as you used to. Your interests change. The things that are important to you may also change. You will have responsibilities that are different from those of most teenagers.

When you become a mother, the way you and the baby's father get along may also change. You might become closer, or you might find that the only thing you have in common is the baby. You may have no relationship at all, especially if he didn't want you to have the baby. It is important to think about this relationship. You need to be realistic about what your life will be like after the baby is born.

The birth of your baby will bring many changes in your life—new responsibilities and new concerns. But now that you know a little more about what becoming a mother will involve, you are better informed and will be better able to make good decisions for you and your baby.

Glossary

anesthesia A substance that causes a loss of feeling in your body.
antibodies Cells produced by the body that can protect it from infection.
bonding Feeling of closeness.
bumper Padded fabric that protects a baby's head from a crib's hard edges.
cervix Entryway of the birth canal.
cesarean section Surgical delivery of a baby.
childbirth The process of having a baby.
colic Sharp pains in a baby's intestines.
contraction Involuntary pushing and releasing of uterus to allow for vaginal delivery of a baby.
fetus Term for unborn baby during last two trimesters.
fontanel Soft spot on top of the baby's head.
formula Liquid food other than breast milk that is fed to a baby.

immunization A shot that protects a person from disease.
labor The physical activities involved in giving birth.
lochia Bloody discharge after childbirth that can last for a week or more.
meconium Dark greenish matter that appears in the first bowel movements of newborn infants.
midwife Health care practitioner who specializes in delivering babies.
nutrients Substances that promote growth and provide nutrition.
obstetrician Doctor who specializes in childbirth.
pediatrician Doctor who specializes in the care of babies and children.
placenta Life-support system for fetus in the uterus.
postpartum depression Feeling of sadness after delivering a baby.
prenatal Before birth.
receiving blanket Blanket used to wrap a baby.
trimester Each three months of pregnancy.
uterus Muscular organ where fetus develops.

Where to Go for Help

The following organizations can refer you to service groups in your area.

American Academy of Pediatrics
141 Northwest Point Boulevard
Elk Grove Village, IL 60007-1098
(847) 434-4000
Web site: http://www.aap.org

American Coalition for Fathers and Children
1718 M Street NW, Suite 187
Washington, DC 20036
(800) 978-DADS (3237)
Web site: http://www.acfc.org

Child Welfare League of America
440 First Street NW, 3rd Floor
Washington, DC 20001-2085
(202) 638-2952
Web site: http://www.cwla.org

For Further Reading

Berlfein, Judy. *Teen Pregnancy*. San Diego: Lucent Books, 1992.

Bode, Janet. *Kids Still Having Kids: Talking About Teen Pregnancy.* Rev. ed. Danbury, CT: Franklin Watts, 1999.

Edeiken, Louise, and Johanna Antar. *Now That You're Pregnant*. New York: Collier Books, 1992.

Eisenberg, Arlene, Sandee E. Hathaway, and Heidi E. Murkoff. *What to Expect When You're Expecting.* 2nd ed. New York: Workman, 1996.

Hess, Mary Abbott, and Anne Elise Hunt. *Eating for Two: The Complete Guide to Nutrition During Pregnancy*. New York: Collier Books, 1992.

Kitzinger, Sheila. *The Year After Childbirth: Surviving and Enjoying the First Year of Motherhood*. New York: Scribner, 1994.

Madaras, Lynda. *My Body, My Self: The "What's Happening to My Body" Workbook for Girls*. New York: Newmarket Press, 1993.

Index

A
active labor, 36
Agency for Child Development, 52
alcohol, dangers of during
   pregnancy, 20, 30

B
bathing your baby, 42
bottle-feeding, 40–41, 56
breast-feeding, 39–41, 56
budget, planning a, 53–54

C
cesarean births, 37
childbirth, stages of, 35–37
child care, finding, 14, 52
Child Support Enforcement
   Program, 51–52
colic, 43–44
colostrum, 24
contractions, 23, 25, 35, 36
cradle cap, 46

D
development of baby, 47–48
diaper rash, 41, 45–46
diapers, 41–42
diet/what to eat, 13, 25–28
diet supplements, 22–23
dilate, definition of, 24, 35
"dropping" of baby, 21, 24
drugs, dangers of during
   pregnancy, 20, 30

E
ear infections in infants, 46
early labor, 35
education/high school, importance
   of, 11, 50
efface, definition of, 24
embryo/fetus, development of,
   18–21
emergencies, 38, 46–47
exercise, 23, 25
expenses, examples of, 50, 53–57

F
family, as source of support, 14–15
father of baby
   change in relationship with, 8, 58
   legal financial obligation of, 15,
      51–52
   as source of support, 15
feeding your baby, 39–41, 43
friendships, changes in, 8, 57–58

G
government/public programs, 11, 50,
   51–52

H
holding your baby, 39, 43, 44

L
labor, stages of, 35–36
labor and delivery, preparing for,
   33–35

Lamaze, 32
lochia, 44

M
meconium, 41
midwife, definition of, 17
morning sickness, 22

O
obstetrician, definition of, 17
Office of Family Assistance (OFA), 51

P
pediatrician, definition of, 45
placenta, 18, 20, 36–37
postnatal care, 37
postpartum depression, 38–39
prenatal care, 17–18, 22
pushing and delivery, 36

S
sleeping of newborns, 41
smoking/tobacco, dangers of during pregnancy, 20, 29–30
support, sources of, 14–16

T
teenage pregnancy
   reasons for, 6–7, 13
   statistics on, 6, 11
Temporary Assistance for Needy Families (TANF), 51
transitional labor, 36
trimesters 19, 21–24, 25

W
weight gain, 22, 23, 25
Women, Infants, Children (WIC), 51

About the Author
Jane Hammerslough is a writer who has worked as a counselor to teenagers on family planning and other women's health issues. Ms. Hammerslough is a graduate of Wesleyan University. She is married and is a mother.

Photo Credits
Cover © Rhoda Sidney/Imageworks; pp. 2, 19, 26, 47 © Custom Medical; p. 9 © Myrleen Cate/Index Stock; pp. 12, 15 © Ron Chapple/FPG; p. 29 © Brian Leng/Corbis; p. 31 © International Stock; p. 34 © Superstock; p. 40 © Mitch Diamond/International Stock.

Design and Layout
Thomas Forget

www.ingramcontent.com/pod-product-compliance
Lightning Source LLC
Chambersburg PA
CBHW041114070526
44584CB00002B/171